MAKE ONLINE DATING WORK FOR YOU

Tips to build a strong profile and meet great people

Written by Sophie Mévisse

Translated by Rebecca Neal

Health and Wellbeing 50MINUTES.com

HEALTH AND WELLBEING
WITHOUT THE HEADACHE

MAKE ONLINE DATING WORK FOR YOU

- **Problem:** at a time when it seems more and more difficult to meet people, the internet seems like the perfect solution. However, finding your soulmate, or at least a stable relationship, online is not always straightforward.
- **Aim:** to discover all the tips you need, as well as common mistakes to avoid, for successful internet dating.
- **FAQs:**
  - What are the advantages and disadvantages of online dating?
  - How much do dating sites cost?
  - Are there other sites that allow you to meet people?
  - Why should I include a profile picture, and how should I choose it?
  - How should I fill out my profile?
  - What rules do I need to follow when talking to people online?
  - When and where should I plan the first date?

If you leave work late and would like to meet new people who share your lifestyle and interests, or if you have had enough of your friends constantly trying to set you up with people you are not interested in, you are far from alone: many people are in the same boat and have turned to the internet to try and meet new people. Whether you are looking for a quick fling or true love, there are a range of options that will let you find new people. There is no time like the present to get started!

WHERE TO MEET PEOPLE

While the decision to meet new people is a straightforward one, choosing the best site for you is much more complicated. Over the past ten years, the number of online dating sites has skyrocketed. Among these many sites, some promise to help you find true love, others make all types of meeting possible, and yet others are geared towards less serious relationships. These sites will also provide you with tools to make your search easier.

The first step is therefore to think about what you are really looking for in this new adventure, so that you can find the site that best suits your personality and what you want.

DATING SITES AND SMARTPHONE APPS

Dating sites are spaces which are entirely dedicated to establishing new relationships. There are different kinds of them, and they target different audiences: some focus on the 20-35 age bracket, while others aim for a social elite, and still others seek to bring together people who share the same passions. This means that you can find everything online, provided you know what you are looking for.

However, it is important to be aware that most of the best-known sites (which therefore have the most singles) will make you pay at some point. They offer subscriptions to allow users to send unlimited messages or see who has been looking at their profile. The money is used to pay for the servers, the interface of the site, and the salaries of the moderators who manage users' profiles. As a general rule, the more successful a site becomes, the more expensive it is to access all the tools it offers. Nonetheless, some try to keep costs down by displaying adverts on the site.

The services offered by subscription packages vary considerably depending on the site and can provide access to sophisticated functions, such as personality tests and horoscopes for your love life, while ensuring users that they can trust the company. Making people pay to access the site allows them to weed out undesirable users such as "fakes" (users with bad intentions who conceal their real identity) and fraudsters.

If you subscribe to a site, do not forget that at the end of your chosen period (one month, six months, a year), the contract will be renewed automatically. You will need to cancel it yourself, or the money will keep going out of your account.

Match.com

Match.com is one of Europe's leading online dating sites, and you have probably already seen one of its many advertisements on television. Although it faces competition from numerous other platforms, which each offer their own unique features and some degree of originality, it is still a benchmark in online dating and has a vast user base of singles of all ages. According to a survey by the French polling organisation TNS Sofres, in 2012 Meetic (Match.com's French counterpart) was the site most recommended by singles.

Although it is free to sign up, you will need to take out a Match subscription if you want to use the email or chat function. However, you can sign up, fill out your profile and contact users who have paid for a subscription for free. When you sign up, you will be able to contact all other users, regardless of whether or not they have paid for a subscription, see who is interested in your profile, enjoy a discount on Match events, and use the site without adverts. One month's subscription costs £29.99, but this goes down to £9.99 per month if you sign up for a six-month subscription. The site also sometimes runs promotions, allowing you to enjoy a discounted subscription if you sign up during a particular window.

Match.com allows you to search for people using basic criteria such as age, location, whether or not the person smokes, and so on. Its simplicity could be a downside for some people who would prefer more detailed information. If this sounds like you, you can sign up for MatchAffinity, which is owned by the same group. This site is discussed in more detail below.

EliteSingles

If you want to meet somebody who is like you, who is as attentive as you and who is as sensitive as you (in short, somebody who will understand you), EliteSingles is the site for you.

When you sign up, you will take a ten-part personality test which measures the five dimensions of your personality (openness, conscientiousness, extraversion, agreeableness and neuroticism), which will then allow you to see how your results match up with those of other profiles. The site will use the information gathered to introduce you to between three and seven compatible matches every day. If you want to get to know somebody better, you can also send the people who have caught your eye a list of questions generated by the site which aim to determine how the other person might react in particular situations.

EliteSingles is a paid service: users cannot send or receive messages without a subscription. A 12-month Premium Comfort subscription will give you the best value for money, at £27.95 per month. If you want to try the site for a limited time, the cost shoots up: £49.95 per month for a three-month Premium Light subscription. These high prices allow the site to select users from the beginning to only target more "demanding" singles.

MatchAffinity

MatchAffinity sees itself as more serious than many other sites, for one simple and good reason: not just anybody can sign up. Unlike on some other sites, the moderators must approve all the photographs that appear on your profile, which means that other users may not be able to view it immediately.

Most of MatchAffinity's users are in the 25-55 age bracket, and many are looking for a serious long-term relationship. These users also tend to be more inclined to invest in a pricy subscription: £44.95 for one month, although you can make big savings if you opt for a six-month package, which works out at £16.95 per month.

Once you join MatchAffinity, you can carry out an advanced search based on criteria such as minimum level of education and smoking habits. The site believes that compatibility is vital to a successful relationship, and claims that its Affinity Questionnaire is an excellent way of ensuring that you and your future partner as well matched.

Tinder

> "Tinder is simple to use. The app gives the user photos. If you find the person attractive, you swipe left on the photo, and if they feel the same about you, you can talk to them. If you aren't interested, all you have to do is swipe right on the photo, and the profile will disappear." (Dylan, 28)

As Dylan explains, Tinder is a smartphone app where both parties have to like the look of one another to start a conversation. The fact that both people have to show an interest is an asset because it allows you to filter out people you are not attracted to. However, the choice is based solely on physical criteria rather than on the personality or interests of the other person. That being said, Tinder makes it easier to meet up in real life, because you are only shown photographs of users who are nearby.

It is nonetheless worth noting that Tinder does not have the best reputation, and many users are not looking for serious or long-term relationships. One journalist has written that "with Tinder, love and seduction become utilitarian. The quality of the conversations plummets and all the magic of seduction disappears, to be replaced by purely functional messages"[1] (Jaillardon, 2015). This statement is confirmed by the results of a survey by the *Institut français d'opinion public* (French Institute of Public Opinion), which showed that the use of dating sites (including dating apps for smartphones) has resulted in two new trends: the emergence of sexual behaviour online (such as exchanging sexual messages or images, which is known as cybersex), and so-called "hookup culture", which involves using communication tools to establish real-life relationships based on sex. In this sense, Tinder is similar to Grindr (an app used by gay men to find partners nearby): its users typically want to find sexual partners rather than a serious relationship. Tinder is therefore recommended for people who are not looking for something serious (at least in theory) but who still want to meet people and have fun. It is also a good way of meeting people near you, whatever the outcome of the date.

Bumble

Bumble is a smartphone app that is particularly popular among younger users. While the principle behind the site is similar to Tinder (swiping left or right to show interest in users, a "match" if both people swipe right), it is unusual among dating sites and apps in that it is designed to enable women to avoid harassment and give them as much control as possible over their dates. This means that women are always the first to send a message in opposite-sex pairings, and must do this within 24 hours or the match will disappear. However, men can still signal their interest by opting

---

1. This quotation has been translated by 50Minutes.com.

to extend the match for a further 24 hours. Even after you have begun talking to someone, it is possible to unmatch the user, block them (so that they cannot see your profile or contact you again) or report them to the app's moderators.

As Bumble targets a young audience, its users' intentions are not always very serious. Having said that, some members are looking for a serious relationship, and there is even an option to search for friends if that is all you are looking for.

The site is intuitive and easy to use: members use their smartphone screen to swipe through profiles and select the ones they are interested in. Although users do not provide detailed information about themselves or fill out a questionnaire, as is the case for some of the other sites in this guide, the app takes information from Facebook, so you can typically see details like a person's age and the university they attended. Users can also upload several photos and write a brief description to accompany their profile.

Bumble is free for both men and women, but it is possible to purchase a premium subscription called Bumble Boost. This allows users to see who is interested in their profile (normally, users are shown profiles with no way of knowing whether the other person is also interested in them) and to re-match with expired connections (meaning matches which disappeared because a message was not sent within 24 hours).

Match and EliteSingles, as well as other popular dating sites such as Plenty Of Fish and OKCupid, have their own smartphone apps. These apps have the main functions of the site: you can send and receive messages, update your personal profile, view other users' profiles, and so on. However, be careful not to purchase too many premium add-ons for these apps, as they can be quite expensive.

SITES FOR SHARED INTERESTS AND SOCIAL NETWORKS

As we mentioned at the start of this guide, the internet offers many possibilities for meeting people. It is therefore entirely possible to meet people on other sites, in particular on sites for shared interests and social networking sites (notably Facebook).

Some people prefer talking to people who have the same interests as them. Forums can therefore be a particularly useful alternative to online dating sites. To find them, all you have to do is type a few key words into a search engine or pay attention to word of mouth. However, these sites require another kind of investment: so that other people can get to know them, users must actively participate in threads in order to become integrated into the community.

Facebook, the most popular social network, allows you to

create and join public or private groups dedicated to a wide range of subjects. Some groups are for shared interests and are a space for conversation, bringing together people who share the same passions. This gives you many opportunities to talk about subjects that you are personally interested in and which you feel comfortable with.

Other groups are linked to particular places: people living in some towns, cities or regions create groups in order to share upcoming events or even photographs of noteworthy places or buildings. This type of group lets you get to know your neighbours and meet people near you. Similarly, if you are abroad, there are many groups for expats of the same nationality to enable you to help and meet each other.

Do not be afraid to go to public events where you could meet people, such as drinks events, exhibitions, lectures or other gatherings. Before you go, you could also look at the profiles of other people who might be attending.

PRACTICAL ADVICE

HOW SHOULD I CHOOSE A USERNAME?

The choice of a username is more significant than you might think. Users will identify you through your username before they know your first name, and your username will help them to decide whether they want to talk to you or not. It is therefore important to choose wisely in order to get people's attention while avoiding certain pitfalls.

According to a study carried out by Queen Mary University of London, playful usernames, meaning those which put the reader in a good mood or those which are funny, are attractive to both sexes. It is therefore important to make sure that your username is "warm" and "happy".

A good username is simple and does not give the impression that it was generated automatically: you should therefore avoid things like strings of numbers, childish usernames or references that will quickly become outdated. It is better to opt for a username inspired by your favourite authors, actors or characters, as this may encourage someone who shares your interests to get in touch with you. Remember that if you choose usernames linked to cultural reference points (band names, directors, film titles, and so on), it is highly likely that fans will talk to you about it, so it would be a shame if you knew nothing about the subject.

You should also choose usernames that are short and easy to pronounce, so that other users can identify you more easily.

WHAT PROFILE PHOTO SHOULD I CHOOSE?

When we sign up to a dating site, we naturally want to look our best because, whatever people might say, physical appearance plays a major part in attraction. While we cannot conceal all our flaws in real life, we may be tempted to make some alterations to our photos to appear in the best possible light online. However, this is a bad idea. When you decide to take your relationship to the next level by arranging to meet in real life, you want to make sure that the other person is not disappointed and does not feel betrayed – and break off the relationship – because you do not look exactly like the photographs on your profile.

> "I had a bad experience with a guy I'd met online a few weeks earlier and who I really liked. We'd arranged to meet and, over the course of the date, I could see that he was disappointed – he had clearly been expecting something else and imagined me differently. On the other hand, I was even more attracted to him than before – he was much better looking than in his photos." (Alex, 27)

Although it is undeniably important, do not forget that our profile picture only shows one fixed, limited aspect of our appearance. This means that, even if the other person has not edited their photograph, you may be surprised the first time you meet them. Bear in mind that many users choose the photographs that they find most flattering for their profile, without this being really representative of the person as a whole.

But how can you choose the right photo? A good mood and happiness are always a winning combination: a smile (as long as it is real and not forced!) will attract a visitor's attention. This is particularly true if you are looking at the viewer of the photo, so it is important to look into the camera. A selfie should not be your first choice, because it seems that men who use them are viewed as less attractive (although this is not the case for women). It is therefore best to use a photograph taken by somebody else to let the other person to get an overall impression of your appearance. Your profile should also feature several photographs of you: a shot of your face as your main photograph, and at least one where your whole body is visible. Finally, as a general rule, it is a good idea to steer clear of too many photographs with your pet.

In summary, a good profile photo should give an idea of your overall appearance, be taken by somebody else, and show you smiling and looking directly at the camera. Finally, although this may seem obvious, you should pay attention to the quality of your photographs. You do not need to use a professional photographer to get good results, but your profile photo absolutely must be clear (avoid arty, out of focus shots) and well composed. Photographs taken with your computer's webcam can work if the quality is good enough, but it is better to use photographs taken with a camera because they tend to be of better quality.

WHAT SHOULD I EMPHASISE IN MY PROFILE?

Your profile is your identity card on the site. It features the information that lets other people find out about you and piques their interest. While profiles are generally set out as a series of short answers to questions about your tastes, your outlook on the world, your appearance, and so on, you are free to write what you want in several spaces: it is up to you to decide what you want to share and to let your creativity show.

The golden rule is to always be yourself and to know yourself well enough to highlight your best features and the things that make you unique (without coming across as vain, of course). Keep it simple and be true to yourself, while at the same time showing your originality. If you do not know how to describe yourself, feel free to ask your friends what they think makes you unique if you feel it will help.

A good profile can be read like a CV: quickly. You need to co-ver everything in a few sentences, while making your reader want to find out more. You do not need 10 000 characters to pique their interest: be clear, concise, brief and direct. In real life, you would not want to meet someone who spent an hour telling you their life story without letting you get a word in edgeways; the same applies on the internet. Users tend to avoid overly lengthy texts. Conversely, they will want to get to know you if you have shared interests, if your profile is funny, or if they like your photographs. It is therefore essential to only highlight things you really like and things that make you unique as a person. You should also consider making your intentions clear by briefly explaining why you joined the site. By indicating your motivations, you can make sure that you only talk to like-minded people. This will prevent any nasty surprises.

A FEW QUICK TIPS

- Be precise: if you like to read, mention your favourite authors and books, or the genres you usually go for. Just saying that you like reading is too vague to spark a conversation.
- Be positive: users are more inclined to start a conversation with people who seem happy and positive, rather than with sad and pessimistic people.
- Try to make your positive features shine through in your description: rather than just saying that you are funny, prove it in your writing with a text that makes people smile.
- Avoid talking about your physical advantages (for example, "I'm a good-looking guy"). This could be viewed as vain; let other people form their own

ideas.
- Proofread everything you write before publishing it in order to eliminate spelling mistakes, as these make people less likely to want to read a message or a profile.

HOW CAN I START A CONVERSATION?

When you send someone a message, take care to make a good first impression. Avoid opening lines like "Hey, how's it going?" Although this is polite and neutral, it may be annoying if you are the tenth person to use it to start a conversation. You should also steer clear of overly simple introductions, like "Steve from London" or "I'm Nathan, what's your name?" These are very mundane and can quickly become boring, especially as many users opt to include their first name and/or the place they are from in their username. If you were talking spontaneously to someone you did not know in real life, you would never introduce yourself by telling them your name followed by where you live. It is more natural to break the ice by saying something about your surroundings before introducing yourself. It is therefore better to start with something funny or by mentioning something you have in common, before moving on to introductions. As well as showing that you are original, which will attract the attention of the person you are contacting, you will preserve a certain mystique, which will pique the other person's curiosity.

You should therefore be original and funny. Show that

you are interesting and interested by the other person by building on a detail in their profile that stood out to you, or even a detail in one of their photos, to start a conversation without going for the easy option.

MAKING THE FIRST MOVE: THE SPECIFICS

You could, for example, highlight a passion that you share with the other person:

- "When I was looking at your profile, I saw that you love [film]. That's one of my favourites too! The part where [...] always gets me."
- "You said in your profile that Iceland is the most beautiful place you've ever travelled to. I haven't had the chance to go yet, but I've heard a lot of good things about it. Is there anything that you'd recommend? Or anything that I should definitely avoid? You never know..."

You can also point out a detail in a photograph:

- "When I was looking at your photos, I saw you were at the [singer or band] concert. You're so lucky that you got to see them live! I wanted to go as well, but it was already sold out. How was it?

Alternatively, you could just try to be funny:

- "I've been desperately looking for something original to say to you, but I'm coming up empty. I don't want to miss the chance to get to know you though!"

Be aware that people will always be happy if you compliment them on their appearance. However, it is not the best way to get into contact with someone else. This approach is often used by sleazy users who can be overly insistent, which gets old quickly. It would also be a shame to only dwell on the physical aspect, especially if a person's profile has interesting information about them: focus instead on their interests, as this will result in a more meaningful conversation.

If somebody does not respond to you immediately even though you can see that they are online, let it go. The person might not want to answer you, or they might just not have had time to get back to you the second you sent the message. The general rule in these situations is to stay calm and not flood their inbox with messages, as this risks driving them away.

WHAT RULES DO I NEED TO FOLLOW WHEN TALKING TO SOMEONE ONLINE?

Even though you are on the internet, it is important to follow a number of safety rules. Never give out personal details such as your surname, your address or your place of work – at least in the early stages of a relationship. You should also avoid giving out confidential information, such as your credit card number.

A good conversation will make you feel good, while a bad one will make you feel uncomfortable. You are under no obligation to keep talking to someone who you do not like or who is bothering you. If the situation gets worse, do not hesitate to contact the site's moderators, who will be able to stop the person from contacting you again. Trust your instincts when talking to someone online.

If the conservation is going well and your instincts are telling you to take things a step further, go for it! You can only get a better idea of someone by meeting them in person.

THE USERS TO AVOID

Overly insistent users

When you start using the site, it is likely that you will soon come across some users who are a little too forward and intrusive for your liking. Fortunately, they are only a minority of users on dating sites. You need to keep in mind that the internet is a haven for shy people and users tend to forget about the impact of their words when they are online. While they would be too afraid of the other person's reaction to begin a real-life conversation by asking highly personal questions, everything is different on the internet: they only have a screen in front of them, which makes it easier to talk about any and every subject.

In most cases, the best solution is to ignore them; they will give up before you do. If they fail to take the hint, feel free to inform a moderator about their behaviour or to block them.

People who are already in a relationship

> "I don't see any difference between a relationship online and a relationship in real life. Maybe it's because I stay honest in both situations, but it wasn't the case for the person I was talking to. She had a boyfriend, but I didn't find out until a few weeks later. Having said that, you could get that kind of surprise in a traditional relationship; it isn't unique to dating sites and apps." (Dylan, 28)

Unfortunately, as Dylan points out, people who are married or already in a relationship do not just crop up on sites dedicated to extramarital encounters. However, some clues can help you to spot them:

- they never log on in the evening or at weekends (because of their family commitments);
- they ask you to only contact them on their mobile, and only at certain times:
- they will meet you anywhere except at their house or apartment.

Scammers

Online fraudsters are a real threat on the internet. It is not always easy to identify them at first, but some elements may draw your attention:

- the person you are talking to writes in very basic English and the tone of your conversations changes considerably from one day to the next (they could be contacting you from abroad, or several people could be writing to you);

- they ask you a lot of questions about your day-to-day life in order to find out about your habits;
- they refuse to meet up, or fail to turn up if you arrange a meeting, but still make sure that they get hold of your phone number, home address, etc.;
- they say contradictory things (one day they have been living somewhere for years; the next day they have never been there) and become attached to you very quickly;
- you cannot find any information about them online (for example, they do not have a Facebook profile).

If you are suspicious about any strange behaviour, get in touch with one of the moderators of the site and stop contacting that person. If the person is blackmailing you, contact the police; blackmail is a criminal offence in the UK.

WHEN AND WHERE SHOULD I PLAN TO MEET IN PERSON?

If, after a few conversations, you feel comfortable and think that the relationship could go further, this means that it is time to move on to the next stage: meeting them in person. Specialists generally recommend meeting in person quite early on. There should only be a few days between the moment when your interest peaks and the date. Once again, the important thing is to listen to your instincts: if you feel ready, go for it; if not, wait a bit longer. There is also no point in rushing the other person, as this is likely to discourage them from meeting you.

Do not forget that, unless you have spoken via webcam, you

do not really know what the other person looks like. You can only get a proper idea about them by meeting them in real life. Furthermore, the more time passes, the more emotionally invested you may become and the more you will feel the need to communicate with the other person in real life.

It is essential to choose the right place and to follow some safety measures:

- Always choose a public place. Why not go for a drink and then head to the cinema?
- Make sure you always tell a friend when and where you are meeting the other person.
- Make sure to always have your mobile phone with you.
- Always make your own way to the place you are meeting: avoid letting the person you are going to meet drive you.

What if the date does not go to plan?

Even if your first messages were promising, there may be no spark between you in real life. These things happen, and there is nothing wrong with that. The important thing is to be honest so that the other person is not under any illusions if they did not feel the same thing as you.

You could also not be attracted to one another, but that does not mean that you should cut off all contact. Even if it is not romantic, your relationship could turn into a great friendship.

> "When I met him, I didn't have feelings for him because I didn't really find him attractive. And the feeling was mutual.

In spite of that, we had a good time together and laughed a lot. Maybe we'll stay in touch and become friends. Who knows?" (Alex, 27)

IN CONCLUSION

Nowadays, it is very easy to meet people on the internet: there are online communities everywhere, and talking to people is easier than ever. The hardest thing is to choose between all the possibilities on offer. The only person who can make this choice is you: it depends on your personality, what you want, and so on. Once you have decided to take the plunge, all you have to do is keep being yourself and come out of your shell as you get to know new people.

And who knows, you might just meet somebody who will change your life...

FAQS

WHAT ARE THE ADVANTAGES AND DISADVANTAGES OF ONLINE DATING?

The internet allows shy people and people who do not have much free time to meet people that they may not be able to find in real life. Although dating sites do everything to make it easier to meet people, you still need to remain vigilant and avoid giving out any personal information.

HOW MUCH DO DATING SITES COST?

Subscription costs vary considerably between sites, but you will always get better rates if you take out a longer subscription. For example, depending on the length of your subscription, the sites in this guide can cost between £9.99 and £49.95 per month. The advantage of subscription services is that, the more expensive they are, the more targeted and serious the users will be.

ARE THERE OTHER SITES THAT ALLOW YOU TO MEET PEOPLE?

You can also use social networking sites like Facebook and Twitter, sites for shared interests (forums) or some smartphone apps (such as Tinder and Bumble).

WHY SHOULD I INCLUDE A PROFILE PICTURE, AND HOW SHOULD I CHOOSE IT?

Your profile photo is essential so that the other person can put a face to your description. It is also proof that you are taking this seriously and that you are not a fake or a fraudster. Ideally, you should choose a recent photograph and, above all, one that is an accurate representation of you, so that the other person is not disappointed. Flash your brightest smile, look at the camera and get someone else to take the photo.

HOW SHOULD I FILL OUT MY PROFILE?

When you are writing your profile, you need to pinpoint and highlight what makes you unique compared to other people, without exaggerating. Making your intentions clear is also always appreciated.

WHAT RULES DO I NEED TO FOLLOW WHEN TALKING TO PEOPLE ONLINE?

Never give out confidential information (full name, bank details, address, and so on) and trust your instincts. If a person seems suspicious to you, feel free to stop talking to them, block them, and/or ask a moderator to get involved.

WHEN AND WHERE SHOULD I PLAN THE FIRST DATE?

As soon as you feel comfortable and ready to move on to the next stage, make a date with the other person. The sooner you go on a date, the sooner you can get a real idea about them. When choosing a location for the date, always opt for a public place (cinema, restaurant, museum), tell a friend where you are going, and make sure that you have your phone with you.

We want to hear from you!
Leave a comment on your online library
and share your favourite books on social media!

FURTHER READING

BIBLIOGRAPHY

- Adams, R. (2015) 7 Drawbacks Of Online Dating, According To Science. *Huffington Post*. [Online]. [Accessed 6 June 2017]. Available from: <http://www.huffingtonpost.com/2015/07/07/online-dating-science_n_7745108.html>
- Carlier, M. (2013) Sites de rencontre: comment identifier les mythos, escrocs et autres losers. *Huffington Post*. [Online]. [Accessed 6 June 2017]. Available from: <http://www.huffingtonpost.fr/2013/05/02/sites-de-rencontre-comment-identifier-les-mythos_n_3199881.html>
- Copeland, L. (2014) The 9 Essential Rules For Writing Your Online Dating Profile. *Huffington Post*. [Online]. [Accessed 6 June 2017]. Available from: <http://www.huffingtonpost.com/lisa-copeland/online-dating-profile_b_5752694.html>
- Duportail, J. (2012) Les «brouteurs d'Abidjan», les nouveaux escrocs d'Internet. *Lefigaro.fr*. [Online]. [Accessed 6 June 2017]. Available from: <http://www.lefigaro.fr/actualite-france/2012/12/07/01016-20121207ARTFIG00560-les-brouteurs-d-abidjan-les-nouveaux-escrocs-d-internet.php>
- Gannac, A.-L. (2011) Internet permet-il de "vraies" histoires ? *Psychologies*. [Online]. [Accessed 6 June 2017]. Available from: <http://www.psychologies.com/Couple/Seduction/L-amour-sur-Internet/Articles-et-dossiers/Internet-permet-il-de-vraies-histoires>

- Gannac, A.-L. (2002) Internet, le choc du premier rendez-vous. *Psychologies*. [Online]. [Accessed 6 June 2017]. Available from: <http://www.psychologies.com/Couple/Seduction/L-amour-sur-Internet/Articles-et-dossiers/Internet-le-choc-du-premier-rendez-vous>
- Izadi, E. (2015) Want to succeed in online dating? Pay more attention to your username. *Washington Post*. [Online]. [Accessed 6 June 2017]. Available from: <https://www.washingtonpost.com/news/the-intersect/wp/2015/02/13/want-to-succeed-in-online-dating-pay-more-attention-to-your-username/?utm_term=.494143b46b6e>
- Jaillardon, K. (2015) De Uber à Tinder, non à l'"ubérisation" de la société ! La séduction n'est pas utilitaire. *L'OBS Le Plus*. [Online]. [Accessed 6 June 2017]. Available from: <http://leplus.nouvelobs.com/contribution/1390368-de-uber-a-tinder-non-a-l-uberisation-de-la-societe-la-seduction-n-est-pas-utilitaire.html>
- Jayat, D. (2013) Chantage à la webcam : j'ai essayé de coincer mon brouteur. *L'Obs Rue 89*. [Online]. [Accessed 6 June 2017]. Available from: <http://tempsreel.nouvelobs.com/rue89/rue89-internet/20131216.RUE0844/chantage-a-la-webcam-j-ai-essaye-de-coincer-mon-brouteur.html>
- Maruani, A. (2015) «Quand t'as rien de mieux à faire, tu vas sur Tinder». *L'Obs Rue 89*. [Online]. [Accessed 6 June 2017]. Available from: <http://tempsreel.nouvelobs.com/rue89/rue89-rue69/20150602.RUE9304/quand-t-as-rien-de-mieux-a-faire-tu-vas-sur-tinder.html>
- Mazaurette, M. (2009) *Osez... les rencontres sur Internet*. Paris: La Musardine.

- Rice, F. (2016) 15 ways to make your online dating profile stand out. *Marie Claire*. [Online]. [Accessed 6 June 2017]. Available from: <http://www.marieclaire.co.uk/life/sex-and-relationships/15-ways-to-make-your-online-dating-profile-stand-out-from-the-pack-1-118673>

Made in the USA
Monee, IL
07 July 2026